Walking The Journey Of Lent:

Reflections on the Scriptures for Cycle B

Richard Gribble, CSC

CSS Publishing Company, Inc.
Lima, Ohio

WALKING THE JOURNEY OF LENT, CYCLE B

FIRST EDITION
Copyright © 2017
by CSS Publishing Co., Inc.

Published by CSS Publishing Company, Inc., Lima, Ohio 45807. All rights reserved. No part of this publication may be reproduced in any manner whatsoever without the prior permission of the publisher, except in the case of brief quotations embodied in critical articles and reviews. Inquiries should be addressed to: CSS Publishing Company, Inc., Permissions Department, 5450 N. Dixie Highway, Lima, Ohio 45807.

Library of Congress Cataloging-in-Publication Data
Names: Gribble, Richard, author.
Title: Walking the journey of Lent : reflections on the scripture for Cycle B / Richard Gribble, CSC.
Description: FIRST EDITION. | Lima : CSS Publishing Company, Inc., 2017. | Includes bibliographical references and index.
Identifiers: LCCN 2017044889 (print) | LCCN 2017047186 (ebook) | ISBN 9780788029196 (eBook) | ISBN 9780788029189 (pbk. : alk. paper)
Subjects: LCSH: Lent--Meditations. | Bible--Meditations. | Common lectionary (1992). Year B. Classification: LCC BV85 (ebook) | LCC BV85 .G7145 2017 (print) | DDC 242/.34--dc23

For more information about CSS Publishing Company resources, visit our website at www.csspub.com, email us at csr@csspub.com, or call (800) 241-4056.

e-book:
ISBN-13: 978-0-7880-2919-6
ISBN-10: 0-7880-2919-3

ISBN-13: 978-0-7880-2918-9
ISBN-10: 0-7880-2918-5

PRINTED IN USA

Contents

Introduction

Steven Spielberg's 1982 motion picture classic *E.T. — The Extra Terrestrial* captured the hearts and minds of moviegoers around the world with its combination of comedy, drama, and tragedy. The plot of the film described E.T.'s quest to "go home" and was framed in the context of the relationship between the visitor from space and his human friend Elliot. E.T., who was left behind accidentally when his spaceship was forced to flee from human intrusion, was lost in a world which could not understand or accept his presence. E.T. knows he will die if he remains in the earth's environment and thus the urgency for him to "phone home" is great. At the end of the movie, when his friends return to earth to retrieve him, there is a sense of triumph that he has met the challenge and now can return home, to a place which will welcome him and in which he can grow to new heights.

E.T.'s trial on earth and his need and desire to go home parallels in many ways the annual opportunity that all Christians can experience during the season of Lent. In her wisdom, the church provides this period of preparation so that we can search our hearts for ways to better prepare ourselves for our ultimate return to the one who made us and fashioned us in God's image. Our preparation during the Lenten season is ostensibly oriented toward the Easter Triduum where we celebrate the passion, death, and resurrection of the Lord, but a broader view shows that this season is a gift which allows special opportunities in our daily life to prepare for our return home to God. Sometimes, like E.T., our communication link with our heavenly home is cut or functions poorly, through lack of use or other problems. Lent is our time to retune our communication system so that we can, as the song from the popular musical *Godspell* says, see God more clearly and strive to follow him to the best of our ability each day.

Lent: A Brief History

The liturgical year we celebrate in Christianity begins with Advent, moves to the celebration of Christmas, continues with

Lent, Easter, and finally concludes with the post-Pentecost Sunday commemorations, developed over time. In the case of Lent, a word derived from the Anglo-Saxon word *lencten*, meaning spring, this evolution begins with the Jewish celebration of Passover and its connection with Jesus' crucifixion and resurrection. While people today presume that the Passover is associated with the story of the Jewish Exodus from Egypt, it is quite probable that the basic concept began before this great event. Biblical scholars suggest that the Jewish Passover was originally a unity of two other celebrations: 1) Passover, a spring sacrifice practiced by nomadic peoples, and 2) Unleavened Bread, a Canaanite agricultural festival adopted by the Hebrews only after their settlement in the promised land.[1] The liturgical historian Thomas Talley suggests that it was in the seventh century BC during the time of King Josiah that the great public festival of Israel's redemption from slavery in Egypt became common, connecting the famous Exodus story with the already existing celebration.[2]

During the time of Jesus, Passover commemorated the Jewish Exodus, but also served as a celebration of hope of the redemption that would be brought by the Messiah. The gospel evangelists tell us that the Passover was the cultic context for Jesus' Last Supper with his apostles. It was during these eight days of the Passover feast that Jesus rose from the dead. Thus, from the outset of Christianity, the association of Passover with Easter as a central feast of the liturgical year was solidified. Yet, the question of when Christians began to observe *Pascha* (Easter) is somewhat questionable. Saint Paul in 1 Corinthians 5:7 seems to indicate that the practice was already common to Christians. He tells his readers that he intends to remain in Ephesus until Pentecost, while referencing Passover, indicating that these were important dates and had a definite meaning for the Corinthians. It seems that the Christian adoption of *Pascha* was a continuation of the Jewish Passover tradition. Still the connection between the Christian and Jewish celebrations is somewhat questionable because the synoptic gospels

1   Unleavened Bread was one of three major Jewish agricultural feasts in Canaan. The other two were the Feast of Weeks (Pentecost) and Tabernacles.

2   Thomas Talley, *The Origins of the Liturgical Year* (New York Pueblo Publishing Company, 1986), p 2.

and John differ on the connection between the Last Supper and Passover.[3] Additionally, conflicts between the Jewish lunar calendar and the Julian solar calendar made observance of a consistent dating for the Christian *Pascha* difficult.[4]

Once the Christian community had definitively established Easter and its centrality to the Church's liturgical celebration, a period of preparation for this festival day was inaugurated. As one might imagine, the nascent Christian community would turn to fasting as a central method to prepare for Jesus' ultimate sacrifice on the cross. The Christian liturgical scholar, Adolph Adam, tells us that the duration of the Lenten fast itself was unclear and, therefore, went through a period of development. Saint Irenaeus, Bishop of Lyons (d. 203), wrote to Pope Victor I commenting on Easter and the differences between East and West practices, but also describes the discrepancy in the pre-Easter fast: "The dispute is not only about the day, but also about the actual character of the fast. Some think that they ought to fast for one day, some for two, and still others for forty consecutive hours. Such variation in the observance did not originated in our own day, but very much earlier in the time of our forefathers."[5] Through a mistranslation, the forty consecutive hours became, by the early second century, forty days. At the first ecumenical Council of the Church, held at Nicaea in 325, the bishops spoke of a *quadragesima* [forty] *pascha* "as something obvious and familiar to all."[6] Saint Athanasius (d. 373) in his "Festal Letters" implored his congregation in Alexandria, Egypt to make a forty day fast prior to the more intense fasting of Holy Week.[7] This forty day "Lenten Period" sought to imitate the forty days Jesus fasted in the desert after his baptism

---

3   John's Gospel casts some doubt whether the Last Supper was actually a Passover meal. John (13:1a) simply states, "Now before the festival of the Passover, Jesus knew that his hour had come to depart from this world and go to the Father." The lack of specificity in the evangelist's words raises some doubts in the minds of scholars.

4   Talley. *Liturgical Year*, 5.

5   Quoted in *New Catholic Encyclopedia*, Volume 8, p 468.

6   Adolph Adam, *The Liturgical Year: Its History & its Meaning After the Reform of the Liturgy* (New York: Pueblo Publishing Company, 1981), p 93.

7   William Saunders, "History of Lent," http://www.catholiceducation.org/en/culture/catholic-contributions/history-of-lent.html

as a personal preparation for his public ministry. It also imitated the forty days Moses fasted on Mount Sinai, the time Elijah fasted on his journey to that same location, and the forty years of Israel's sojourn in the desert on their return to the promised land.[8]

Determining a forty-day period of preparation itself had an evolutionary genesis. The Lenten preparation period originally began on the sixth Sunday before Easter and lasted until Maundy (Holy) Thursday. However, because Sundays, as celebrations of the resurrection, could not be days of fast, modifications to this original time period were necessary to achieve forty days of Lent. This was achieved in two different steps. First, Good Friday and Holy Saturday were separated from the Triduum and added to the preparatory period, leading to 36 days of fast. Secondly, during the reign of Pope Gregory the Great (590-604), four days prior to the first Sunday of Lent were added, leading to the start of Lent on Ash Wednesday, and achieving the forty day fast.

Fasting and penitence, two of the important themes of Lent, developed once the forty-day period of preparation was set. Initially, the Lenten fast required the faithful to eat only one single daily meal, usually taken in the evening. Later, abstinence from meat and wine was added; later still, dairy products were added to the prohibited list. After the high medieval era, however, a certain relaxation of this regimen was made in line with the higher esteem accorded the human body. Penitents initiated their reentry into the community of the faithful on Ash Wednesday by wearing special penitential garments and sprinkling ashes on themselves as an expression of sorrow and repentance. Jesus refers to this process in Matthew 11:21, relating it to an ancient custom of the Hebrews: "If the mighty works done in you had been done in Tyre and Sidon, they would have repented long ago in sackcloth and ashes." The early church fathers, Tertullian and Cyprian, say this practice was familiar to the early church as well. Although public ecclesiastical penance disappeared by the end of the first millennium, the rite of using ashes was retained and was applied to all the faithful, not penitents alone.

8   Adam, *Liturgical Year*, pp 91-94.

Lent Today

The season of Lent is a special time when Christians make an extra effort to ready themselves for the Paschal mystery; the passion, death, and resurrection of Jesus Christ. It's a time of preparation given to us to shake off the lethargy that sometimes creeps into our lifestyle and to renew once again our commitment to the Christian way of life. Lent is a time in some ways to prepare ourselves for the ultimate journey home. As E.T. prepared himself to "go home," we must ready ourselves for Easter, as well as our ultimate return to God.

From the tradition of the church we have certain areas that are annually given some emphasis in this Lenten time of preparation. We think especially of fasting, prayer, and almsgiving. The church asks us to reflect upon these virtues and to see where we can improve or make a greater contribution. One way that the church helps us in this quest for greater perfection, in imitation of Jesus, is through the scriptures used in the Revised Common Lectionary. Many of the aspects of fasting, prayer, and almsgiving are seen in the six-week journey of faith that is Lent.

The centrality of scripture and its message that brings both challenges and hope must be the foundation upon which we build our Lenten preparation. Liturgical Year B provides a rich set of biblical readings that can assist us to grow in our spiritual lives. The centerpiece for this particular celebration is set on Ash Wednesday when we are encouraged to return home, that is, our spiritual home with God. The forty day Lenten season gives us numerous opportunities to prepare ourselves for this important homecoming. Along the road of returning home we are challenged in many ways.

First, we realize that life throws us many curves, obstacles, and detours and, thus, we must be ready for such tests; there is nothing to fear. We are next called to seek transformation in our life, realizing that such significant change will help us grow in the positive ways we need. We are called as well to restore our relationship with God, realizing that while at times we may think it possible, it is impossible to fool God. Thus, we need to restore our relationship with the one who gave us life. Cognizant of our need to restore this relationship, we next must seek the light which only Christ can bring. Too often we seek the light of secular society, but it is only the light of Jesus that will direct us to our true home. Lastly, we are challenged to sacrifice, to die to self in some small way so that others who do not enjoy the daily benefits of life that are the norm for most of us may have at least something. If we can do these things, then when Easter Sunday arrives, we will be able to see and believe: to see that the tomb is empty and to believe that the Lord has risen. This is only possible, however, if we have cleared out sufficient space in our hearts so that the risen Lord can find a place to abide.

It is my hope that this Lenten Bible study can be a helpful and effective way for groups and individuals to reflect upon the scriptures and through this process better prepare ourselves for the greatest of all celebrations, Easter, when Jesus rises from the dead and brings all Christians the possibility of salvation. Like any effort in life that is meritorious, this Bible study will require some effort, but it need not and should not be a burden. Rather, in sharing with others, and allowing the Spirit of God to flow through us, we can come to greater insights as to what the scriptures might mean for us and how, most importantly, we can apply them to our lives. Thus, I encourage you to allow the word of God to challenge you as you engage it in a friendly environment with others who seek to walk the same path toward greater holiness. It is the Lord Jesus we seek and his kingdom we need to build. Let us do our share by walking this important journey with him, from triumph, to death, to resurrection and to eternal life.

Reverend Richard Gribble, CSC, Ph.D.

Ash Wednesday
Theme: Coming Home

Opening Prayer:

O Lord, our God, today we, your sons and daughters, begin this great season of grace, Lent, when we, like your son, Jesus, journey to the desert to prepare our hearts and minds for the celebration of the Paschal mystery, Christ's passion, death, and resurrection. Our busy lives in this contemporary world often do not allow us the opportunity to slow down and to contemplate those things that are most important, especially our relationship with you. Periodically in our lives we go home, to the place of our original family, to rest, to relax, and to re-energize ourselves for the daily grind that is modern life. Similarly, we pray that this special forty day period of prayer will be our opportunity to return home to our Christian roots, allowing us to re-energize ourselves for the battle against the forces of evil. Jesus showed us the example of a prayerful life lived in the presence of God. Let us, as we begin this journey by opening ourselves to the possibilities God sends our way, make our Lenten journey one that will be fulfilling in every way. Amen.

Additional prayers of the group

Lesson I: Joel 2:1-2, 12-17

Blow the trumpet in Zion; sound the alarm on my holy mountain! Let all the inhabitants of the land tremble, for the day of the Lord is coming, it is near, a day of darkness and gloom, a day of clouds and thick darkness! Like blackness there is spread upon the mountains a great and powerful people; their like has never been from of old, nor will be again after them through the years of all generations… "Yet even now," says the Lord, "return to me with all your heart, with fasting, with weeping, and with mourning; and rend your hearts and not your garments. "Return to the Lord, your God, for he is gracious and merciful, slow to anger, and abounding in steadfast love, and repents of evil. Who knows whether he will not turn and repent, and leave a blessing behind him, a cereal offering and a drink offering for the Lord, your God? Blow the trumpet in Zion; sanctify a fast; call a solemn assembly; gather the people. Sanctify the congregation; assemble the elders; gather the children, even nursing infants. Let the bridegroom leave his room, and the bride her chamber. Between the vestibule and the altar let the priests, the ministers of the Lord, weep and say, "Spare thy people, O Lord, and make not thy heritage a reproach, a byword among the nations. Why should they say among the peoples, 'Where is their God?'"

(Or Isaiah 58:1-12)

"Cry aloud, spare not, lift up your voice like a trumpet; declare to my people their transgression, to the house of Jacob their sins. Yet they seek me daily, and delight to know my ways, as if they were a nation that did righteousness and did not forsake the ordinance of their God; they ask of me righteous judgments, they delight to draw near to God. 'Why have we fasted, and thou seest it not? Why have we humbled ourselves, and thou takest no knowledge of it?' Behold, in the day of your fast you seek your own pleasure, and oppress all your workers. Behold, you fast only to quarrel and to fight and to hit with wicked fist. Fasting like yours this day will not make your voice to be heard on high. Is such the fast that I choose, a day for a man to humble himself?

Is it to bow down his head like a rush, and to spread sack-cloth and ashes under him? Will you call this a fast, and a day acceptable to the Lord? "Is not this the fast that I choose: to loose the bonds of wickedness, to undo the thongs of the yoke, to let the oppressed go free, and to break every yoke? Is it not to share your bread with the hungry, and bring the homeless poor into your house; when you see the naked, to cover him, and not to hide yourself from your own flesh? Then shall your light break forth like the dawn, and your healing shall spring up speedily; your righteousness shall go before you, the glory of the Lord shall be your rear guard. Then you shall call, and the Lord will answer; you shall cry, and he will say, Here I am. If you take away from the midst of you the yoke, the pointing of the finger, and speaking wickedness, if you pour yourself out for the hungry and satisfy the desire of the afflicted, then shall your light rise in the darkness and your gloom be as the noonday. And the Lord will guide you continually, and satisfy your desire with good things, and make your bones strong; and you shall be like a watered garden, like a spring of water, whose waters fail not. And your ancient ruins shall be rebuilt; you shall raise up the foundations of many generations; you shall be called the repairer of the breach, the restorer of streets to dwell in."

Lesson II: 2 Corinthians 5:20b-6:10

We beseech you on behalf of Christ, be reconciled to God. For our sake he made him to be sin who knew no sin, so that in him we might become the righteousness of God. Working together with him, then, we entreat you not to accept the grace of God in vain. For he says, "At the acceptable time I have listened to you, and helped you on the day of salvation." Behold, now is the acceptable time; behold, now is the day of salvation. We put no obstacle in any one's way, so that no fault may be found with our ministry, but as servants of God we commend ourselves in every way: through great endurance, in afflictions, hardships, calamities, beatings, imprisonments, tumults, labors, watching, hunger; by purity, knowledge, forbearance, kindness, the Holy Spirit, genuine love, truthful speech, and the power of God; with the weapons of righteousness for the right hand and for the left; in honor and dishonor, in ill repute and good repute. We are treated as impostors, and yet are true; as unknown, and yet well known; as dying, and behold we live; as punished, and yet not killed; as sorrowful, yet always rejoicing; as poor, yet making many rich; as having nothing, and yet possessing everything.

Gospel: Matthew 6:1-6, 16-21

"Beware of practicing your piety before men in order to be seen by them; for then you will have no reward from your Father who is in heaven. Thus, when you give alms, sound no trumpet before you, as the hypocrites do in the synagogues and in the streets, that they may be praised by men. Truly, I say to you, they have received their reward. But when you give alms, do not let your left hand know what your right hand is doing, so that your alms may be in secret; and your Father who sees in secret will reward you… And when you pray, you must not be like the hypocrites; for they love to stand and pray in the synagogues and at the street corners, that they may be seen by men. Truly, I say to you, they have received their reward. But when you pray, go into your room and shut the door and pray to your Father who is in secret; and your Father who sees in secret will reward you. And when you fast, do not look dismal, like the hypocrites, for they disfigure their faces that their fasting may be seen by men. Truly, I say to you, they have received their reward. But when you fast, anoint your head and wash your face, that your fasting may not be seen by men but by your Father who is in secret; and your Father who sees in secret will reward you. Do not lay up for yourselves treasures on earth, where moth and rust consume and where thieves break in and steal, but lay up for yourselves treasures in heaven, where neither moth nor rust consumes and where thieves do not break in and steal. For where your treasure is, there ,will your heart be also."

Reflection:
Coming Home

The opportunity to go home is an experience for which all people wait and prepare. Going home, whether this means a return to the place of our birth, the house where we grew up, or even our homecoming after a vacation, business trip or a year at college, does not happen without laying some groundwork. For some people all that may be necessary is a phone call informing those at home that you are on the way. Others might have to plan a trip, considering time, money, and method if the distance to be traveled is great. At times, the experience of going home is fraught with apprehension because of previous events, strained relationships, unanswered questions, or uncertainty of reception. If we return home it is necessary to wait and make arrangements; we must prepare ourselves, each person in a different way.

Ultimately, the sole reason that God created us and the only truly important goal in our lives must be to return home to God. Along the road, God showers us with multiple and varied gifts, plus opportunities, and asks us to contribute to the building of the kingdom in our world. We participate in this effort individually and collectively by leading lives of discipleship and holiness, placing ourselves at the service of one another, especially the lowly and those unable to repay our efforts. God has much for us to do, but all our labors point toward the final goal of union with the Creator, the source of all life and goodness.

Lent, our annual season of grace which gives us the opportunity to prepare ourselves to return home, begins this day by asking us to look into our hearts in order to determine what we need most in getting ready for our homecoming with the Lord. The prophet Joel tells us, "Rend your hearts, not your garments, and return to the Lord, your God." He proclaims that the trumpet is to be blown and the people gathered; they are to awake and begin the inner journey of self-reflection. Preparation for our journey home must begin with a self-evaluation of the heart. Some of what we discover on the inward search will please us because it is of God and holy, but other things will disappoint us, especially when we realize that our own lack of effort, refusal to listen, or inability to love has cast darkness on our souls. Our self-discovery may require us to mend a fence or two along the road.

Fortunately, it is through such an inner journey that we come to the knowledge of our need to be reconciled to self, one another, and finally to God. Paul tells the Corinthians, "Be reconciled to God!" Jesus Christ, the Word incarnate, understands our human frailty and knows our need for reconciliation. It is the Lord who took the journey of introspection many times — a night in prayer to the Father, his temptation at the hand of Satan, and his agony in the Garden of Gethsemane — all in preparation to return to God who sent him. Jesus' experience, his own private Lent, his preparation for Calvary, must be our example as we make this special journey during this season of grace.

Once we look inside, discover and accept ourselves, and then find reconciliation, we are ready for the discipline which Lent asks of us. Traditionally, as Matthew's gospel suggests, using Jesus' words, the church finds its discipline in the areas of almsgiving, fasting, and prayer. Giving from the heart and not just the mind is what true charity asks of us. To be an almsgiver necessitates our dedication but it also requires our reflection on why we do what we do—for self or for the Lord? Fasting and prayer can be conducted in public ways, but again, who are we trying to impress? As Matthew says, God sees in the privacy of the heart which is all that is truly important.

The journey of Lent has begun and so too our preparation for the journey home. Whether God calls tonight or in seventy years, our preparation must be true and sincere. Let us, as this special season begins, look into our hearts, seek reconciliation, with self, others, and God, and then begin to discipline ourselves for this journey to death, resurrection, and in the end, eternal life.

Discussion Questions:

1. As I begin my journey of Lent, what avenues of my life need to be widened and straightened in order to properly find the presence of God all around me?

2. When I think of coming home to God, what do I need to prepare for the journey that I undertake?

3. What areas of my life need to be reconciled in order to properly and freely walk the journey of Lent?

4. At the outset of this journey, what fears or apprehensions exist inside me that may prevent me from engaging fully in this sacred season of grace?

5. What are my goals for Lent? What do I hope to achieve and/or gain?

Concluding Prayer:

God our loving Father, we begin this holy season of Lent by considering the preparations we must make to properly return home to you and your son, Jesus. Remove all fears, apprehensions, and barriers that prevent us from walking this road with our brothers and sisters. Help us to negotiate the hurdles and obstacles that society often throws in our path, and allow us to continue on the road. Grant us the time, the patience, and the opportunity we need to always keep our priorities straight and to actively engage the challenges that this season brings. Make us aware of what we must do, at the outset of our journey, to properly and faithfully follow in the footsteps of your son, Jesus, who showed us the path of life and models for us the way to live for others. Amen.

Lent 1
Theme: Don't Fear The Wait

Opening Prayer

O Lord, our God, as we begin in earnest the journey of Lent, we ask you to open our hearts and minds to the possibilities and opportunities you bring. Too often we assume that only what we believe to be good, positive, and profitable can come from you, and we fail to understand or realize that at times challenges are sent our way by your hand. Help us to understand what we can gain from the various challenges and obstacles that life brings. Give us the strength to meet these challenges head-on and to avoid the easy road that might seek to avoid or even negate the opportunities such challenges can bring. We realize that Lent is a time to recollect our thoughts, ideas, and opinions, and to seek ways to orient them in more positive ways for the benefit of God and his people, the church. May the journey we now fully engage, O Lord, be for us the way to find new avenues to deepen our own spirituality, to discover new ways of assisting others, and through these means, to draw closer to you in all we do and say. Amen.

Additional prayers of the group

Lesson I: Genesis 9:8-17

Then God said to Noah and to his sons with him, "Behold, I establish my covenant with you and your descendants after you, and with every living creature that is with you, the birds, the cattle, and every beast of the earth with you, as many as came out of the ark. I establish my covenant with you, that never again shall all flesh be cut off by the waters of a flood, and never again shall there be a flood to destroy the earth." And God said, "This is the sign of the covenant which I make between me and you and every living creature that is with you, for all future generations: I set my bow in the cloud, and it shall be a sign of the covenant between me and the earth. When I bring clouds over the earth and the bow is seen in the clouds, I will remember my covenant which is between me and you and every living creature of all flesh; and the waters shall never again become a flood to destroy all flesh. When the bow is in the clouds, I will look upon it and remember the everlasting covenant between God and every living creature of all flesh that is upon the earth." God said to Noah, "This is the sign of the covenant which I have established between me and all flesh that is upon the earth."

Lesson II: 1 Peter 3:18-22

 For Christ also died for sins once for all, the righteous for the unrighteous, that he might bring us to God, being put to death in the flesh but made alive in the spirit; in which he went and preached to the spirits in prison, who formerly did not obey, when God's patience waited in the days of Noah, during the building of the ark, in which a few, that is, eight persons, were saved through water. Baptism, which corresponds to this, now saves you, not as a removal of dirt from the body but as an appeal to God for a clear conscience, through the resurrection of Jesus Christ, who has gone into heaven and is at the right hand of God, with angels, authorities, and powers subject to him.

Gospel: Mark 1:9-15

In those days Jesus came from Nazareth of Galilee and was baptized by John in the Jordan. And when he came up out of the water, immediately he saw the heavens opened and the Spirit descending upon him like a dove; and a voice came from heaven, "Thou art my beloved Son with thee I am well pleased." The Spirit immediately drove him out into the wilderness. And he was in the wilderness forty days, tempted by Satan; and he was with the wild beasts; and the angels ministered to him.

Now after John was arrested, Jesus came into Galilee, preaching the gospel of God, and saying, "The time is fulfilled, and the kingdom of God is at hand; repent, and believe in the gospel."

Reflection:
Don't Fear the Wait

Carlo Rienzi had never been tested. He was an attorney but he had no mission, no case. He was fearful and apprehensive; he did not want the trial that he knew must come. The case came but it seemed an impossible task. A young woman had shot the mayor of a small village without provocation, at least so it seemed on the surface. Carlo was assigned by the court as the woman's legal defense. The evidence was overwhelming. The people in the town had loved their mayor; they could see no reason why he was killed. The whole town was against Carlo and his client. Although it was the woman who faced the jury, the trial for Carlo may have been greater. It was a test of his character. Could he perform as he had been trained; would he hold up under the pressure? The trial was a test of his will as well. In the face of overwhelming adversity, could he stay with his client and give her a fair and complete defense?

Although the evidence was against him, Carlo's perseverance would win the day. The trial took place in a small court room in the village where the crime had been committed. Carlo went to the place of the trial in order to find himself. In his investigation, Carlo Rienzi found a reason for the young woman's actions. He discovered that the mayor was not the kind and gentle man that most people in the village knew; he had a mysterious past. In the end, Carlo's client was convicted but she received the least sentence possible for the crime. Carlo Rienzi, as a lawyer had been tested and found worthy.

Morris West's novel *Daughter of Silence* tells the story of the trial of a man and how he found himself through that experience. Lent is a time when we are tested and challenged to find ourselves and experience our faith in greater and fuller ways. In the gospel, Jesus goes to the desert to find himself, to discover his mission in life. While in the desert, he is put to the test by Satan. The trial is a series of temptations to all the allurements of this world. Jesus survives the period of his trial; he is found worthy. Angels come to wait on him. Jesus is now ready to go forth and perform his mission. His message is clear, "Reform your lives, the reign of God is near."

God has tested the world as well. In the first lesson, we hear that the world's people were evil; they refused to listen to God. Therefore, the great flood was sent because the world was not up to the test of God. Yet, some people had remained faithful. Noah and his family lived in God's presence; they survived their period of trial. Because of the faithfulness to Noah, God made a covenant with humankind — never again would the world be destroyed by a great flood.

In our daily lives, God sets before us many challenges, many situations which appear to be great trials. Like Jesus' journey to the desert, our Lenten journey, if accepted properly, will be a great challenge, a desert experience. The challenge we will face will make us better people, more full and complete. In Morris West's novel, Carlo Rienzi made something of himself through meeting the challenge head on, by succeeding in his own personal trial of mind and perseverance. Similarly, Jesus became perfect, as the letter to the Hebrews tells us, through suffering, his own personal trial. Our lives are filled with trials. There are challenges at work with our business associates, with the boss, with our duties. There are challenges at school, with classmates, teachers, and homework assignments. There are trials and challenges in life, with problems, illness, suffering, and death.

How do we handle all these trials, these challenges from God? The answer is to go, like Carlo Rienzi and Jesus, to the desert. The solution will be found there. The solutions to life's trials are found in prayer, works of mercy, and fasting, the traditional Lenten observances. None of these works change God — for the Lord, as we know, is all knowing, all loving, and immutable. But through prayer, works of mercy, and fasting, *we* change. We can then accept the trials and challenges of life. More importantly, we can accept God's will in our lives. Through trial and challenge we grow; through prayer we learn acceptance.

We begin the Lenten journey by traveling to the desert. It is a journey of trial and challenge. Even though this journey may be difficult, we believe that the challenge allows us to grow and accept the will of God in our lives. Today, therefore, let us seek the challenge of the desert. Let us turn to God in prayer; let us be transformed on our personal journey to Calvary and resurrection.

Discussion Questions:

1. How do I deal with adversity in my life? When problems arise, where do I go for answers?

2. Do I have the patience to work out answers to challenges I face or am I always looking for simple solutions?

3. When the burdens and problems of others impact my life, what has been my reaction? Do I run from the situation or do I give support and assistance?

4. What are the most important lessons I have learned in life from times when I experienced failure or defeat?

5. When God calls me to go in a different direction or to accept a new challenge, what has been my reaction? Do I have the courage to accept the invitations that come from God?

Concluding Prayer:

God our heavenly Father, we thank you for the opportunity to draw closer to you as we initiate with full vigor our study of the scriptures during this Lenten season. We all experience various burdens, failures, difficulties, and obstacles in life. If we understand that there is nothing to fear, but rather with your assistance and grace, see these as opportunities to grow in holiness, then we will be that much more ready in the future to negotiate and endure such trials. Our readings and reflections on this first Sunday in Lent have helped us to understand that while every day will not be filled with light and joy, all days, which are indeed gifts from you, can be opportunities to grow and strengthen ourselves for the journey ahead. May we always see in the various trials of life the opportunity to find you and your son Jesus, the one who died to set us free and will always be our brother, Savior, and Lord. Amen.

Theme: Trust Necessitates Sacrifice

Opening Prayer:

Good and gracious God, we open our hearts and minds to you once again to continue our journey along the Lenten path. We seek to come with the hope that what we read, study, and the conversations in which we engage, will be fruitful in helping us to walk this journey more graciously and faithfully. We live in a world where we often have experiences that challenge our faith. It may be a problem in our family, a challenge at work, some difficulty in our neighborhood, or even a feeling that God somehow has abandoned us. As we hear about the faith of Abraham and that of the apostles on Mount Tabor, help us to always find the good and positive things that can be found from all the challenges that come our way. Let us remain open to the possibilities they present. May our study this week help us to be more open to challenges and bring us greater trust in the Lord. In this way, we can follow the plan you have mapped out for us, and be secure that we always rest in the palm of your hand. Amen.

Additional prayers of the group

Lesson I: Genesis 17:1-7, 15-16

When Abram was ninety-nine years old the Lord appeared to Abram, and said to him, "I am God Almighty; walk before me, and be blameless. And I will make my covenant between me and you, and will multiply you exceedingly." Then Abram fell on his face; and God said to him, "Behold, my covenant is with you, and you shall be the father of a multitude of nations. No longer shall your name be Abram, but your name shall be Abraham; for I have made you the father of a multitude of nations. I will make you exceedingly fruitful; and I will make nations of you, and kings shall come forth from you. And I will establish my covenant between me and you and your descendants after you throughout their generations for an everlasting covenant, to be God to you and to your descendants after you."… And God said to Abraham, "As for Sarai your wife, you shall not call her name Sarai, but Sarah shall be her name. I will bless her, and moreover I will give you a son by her; I will bless her, and she shall be a mother of nations; kings of peoples shall come from her."

Lesson II: Romans 4:13-25

The promise to Abraham and his descendants, that they should inherit the world, did not come through the law but through the righteousness of faith. If it is the adherents of the law who are to be the heirs, faith is null and the promise is void. For the law brings wrath, but where there is no law there is no transgression. That is why it depends on faith, in order that the promise may rest on grace and be guaranteed to all his descendants — not only to the adherents of the law but also to those who share the faith of Abraham, for he is the father of us all, as it is written, "I have made you the father of many nations"— in the presence of the God in whom he believed, who gives life to the dead and calls into existence the things that do not exist. In hope he believed against hope, that he should become the father of many nations; as he had been told, "So shall your descendants be." He did not weaken in faith when he considered his own body, which was as good as dead because he was about a hundred years old, or when he considered the barrenness of Sarah's womb. No distrust made him waver concerning the promise of God, but he grew strong in his faith as he gave glory to God, fully convinced that God was able to do what he had promised. That is why his faith was "reckoned to him as righteousness." But the words, "it was reckoned to him," were written not for his sake alone, but for ours also. It will be reckoned to us who believe in him that raised from the dead Jesus our Lord, who was put to death for our trespasses and raised for our justification.

Gospel: Mark 8:31-38

And he began to teach them that the son of man must suffer many things, and be rejected by the elders and the chief priests and the scribes, and be killed, and after three days rise again. And he said this plainly. And Peter took him, and began to rebuke him. But turning and seeing his disciples, he rebuked Peter, and said, "Get behind me, Satan! For you are not on the side of God, but of men." And he called to him the multitude with his disciples, and said to them, "If any man would come after me, let him deny himself and take up his cross and follow me. For whoever would save his life will lose it; and whoever loses his life for my sake and the gospel's will save it. For what does it profit a man, to gain the whole world and forfeit his life? For what can a man give in return for his life? For whoever is ashamed of me and of my words in this adulterous and sinful generation, of him will the Son of man also be ashamed, when he comes in the glory of his father with the holy angels."

Or Mark 9:2-9

And after six days Jesus took with him Peter and James and John, and led them up a high mountain apart by themselves; and he was transfigured before them, and his garments became glistening, intensely white, as no fuller on earth could bleach them. And there appeared to them Elijah with Moses; and they were talking to Jesus. And Peter said to Jesus, "Master it is well that we are here; let us make three booths, one for you and one for Moses and one for Elijah." For he did not know what to say, for they were exceedingly afraid. And a cloud overshadowed them, and a voice came out of the cloud, "This is my beloved son; listen to him." And suddenly looking around they no longer saw any one with them but Jesus only. And as they were coming down the mountain, he charged them to tell no one what they had seen, until the son of man should have risen from the dead.

Reflection:
Trust Necessitates Sacrifice

In the mid-nineteenth-century, Africa, that mysterious land known unfortunately in past generations as the Dark Continent, was beginning to open to the western world. One of the great mysteries that the continent held was the source of the great River Nile, known at the time as a significant river, but today as the world's longest. Was there a high mountain range in the interior of the continent that, despite its proximity to the equator, was snow-capped year round and provided a water source? Was there a series of tributaries that fed into the one River Nile? Was there some large body of water that was the source? One brave British explorer, John Henning Speke, a man who was willing to sacrifice, to accept the ridicule of others, yet with total confidence in his ability and in God, would be the one to solve this great mystery.

Speke was born in Somerset, England on May 4, 1827. An adventurer all his life, he, along with a companion, Sir Richard Francis Burton, explored the wilds of the eastern tip of the African continent, an area today known as Somalia, in the first years of the 1850s. It was the great mystery of the source of the Nile, however, that captivated Speke. Thus, after serving in the Crimean War, Speke and Burton set out in June 1857 to find the answer. They left from Zanzibar and traveled north and west through the interior of the continent. In early 1858, they discovered Lake Tanganyika, certainly a significant body of water, but not one from which any major rivers flowed. Both men fell ill, but John Henning Speke recovered sufficiently to continue his trek north. After several months, he discovered an even greater inland water source, which he called Nyanza or Lake Victoria, after the reigning British queen. Speke was certain that this must the source of the Nile, but he did not find the definite source and his former partner, Burton, was doubtful.

Not to be deterred in his quest, despite the skepticism of many, Speke in 1860, with a new companion, James Grant, organized an expedition to survey the north and western sections of

Lake Victoria. In 1862 they discovered the source of some great river, although they were not certain if it was the Nile. The two men continued to follow the river north to a village called Gondokoro, a place where a fellow British adventurer, Samuel Baker, had reached in following the Nile south. Thus, it was now certain, the great mystery of the source of the Nile had been solved.

The discovery of the source of the River Nile, told in the fascinating book, *White Nile*, is a story of courage, sacrifice, and trust. Today, as we continue our Lenten journey, our readings from scripture challenge us to demonstrate trust, realizing that the sacrifice we make to find God's kingdom is worth every ounce of our efforts.

Can any of us imagine the faith and trust shown by Abraham? Originally named Abram, this man was asked by God to leave the country of his birth, to abandon his heritage, livelihood, and friends, and to travel to a distant land. This request came from a God he did not know or understand. Yet, somehow he managed to summon the faith, despite the hardship it would require, and moved with his wife from Ur to what would become the promised land of Israel. In today's first lesson, we hear that the same Abraham is now asked to have sufficient faith: that even though he is 99 years old and his wife is beyond childbearing age, he will be given a son, that he will actually have progeny and be the father of a great nation, as this mysterious God had promised from the outset. Certainly Abraham's faith was placed on trial, but he passed the test. Saint Paul, in today's second lesson, reminds the Romans, a Christian community he had not founded, but hoped to visit, that their faith must be like Abraham, never doubting and willing to undergo significant trials. Certainly that would be the case when the infamous Roman persecutions would arise in succeeding years and centuries.

Most people thought that John Henning Speke's quest for the source of the Nile was folly, but he disregarded the doubters and continued to pursue his dream. He, like Abraham in God, had complete confidence and trust. We today do not have the advantage of the Transfiguration event. Unlike Peter, James, and John, we will not see the Lord transfigured before our eyes and thus in an overt way be convinced that we should have confidence in God. But, it is such faith that is the daily challenge of being a Christian. We need, each and every day, to cast out the darkness generated by fear, sin and ignorance, and replace this with the light of trust, righteous acts, and knowledge. Many challenges will come our way and we will be asked to sacrifice — to go somewhere we would rather not go, to do something we would rather not do, to undergo some trial that we would rather not experience. But we know, as John Henning Speke demonstrated in history, and Abraham and God show us in the scriptures, that we must trust and have faith. Our trust must be strong and oriented correctly. The tendency is to have too much faith in ourselves and to place all our hope in the world which is so inviting. Ultimately, however, the trust and faith we need must be in God. The author of the book of Proverbs, chapter 3, puts it well: "Trust in the Lord always, on your own intelligence rely not." May we take up the challenge and sacrifice as necessary in order to find greater faith in God.

Discussion Questions:

1. How can this Lenten experience transform me in my efforts to be more Christlike in all I say and do?

2. What needs to be changed in my life? What things do I need to root out as inconsistent with my relationship with God?

3. How have I experienced and responded to challenges of trust in my life? Have I seen these as opportunities to move and grow or as obstacles to be avoided?

4. Am I more attuned to the external things of life, the visible and tangible, or do I have the strength to look to those spiritual things which are more lasting, although they are invisible and intangible?

5. How do I react to and be supportive to those in our lives, family members, neighbors, colleagues at work, who are experiencing transition in their lives? What can I do to walk the road with them?

Concluding Prayer:

Lord Jesus, Son of the Father, through the lessons we have studied and discussed this week you teach us to trust more firmly and fully in you. You also teach us through your Transfiguration for a moment in time to seek permanent transformation in our own lives. Help us to always trust you fully and not be afraid of the various transitions and possibilities in life, for they bring us the opportunity to experience a deeper and more intimate relationship with you. Too often we seek answers in the material world, whether that is our physical appearance, our financial status, or our position in society. Grant us the grace to understand that such temporary transitions are false answers to the question of what we need more permanently, namely, to always be close to you. May the opportunities you give to us in our daily lives be transformational, whether it be something minor or more significant, and allow them to be accepted by us as ways to grow in holiness, giving us the strength to serve you and your people more fully and completely each and every day of our lives. Amen.

Theme: You Can't Fool God

Opening Prayer:

O God Father, Son, and Holy Spirit, we once again gather together in your name to continue our study of scripture and to be nurtured by it. As we draw near to the midpoint of our Lenten journey, we know that, while we may have accomplished some of our goals, we are far from where we need and want to be in order to worthily celebrate the great Paschal mystery: the passion, death, and resurrection of Jesus. You sent your son into the world to show us how to live and to set us free. Help us, as we discuss your holy word, to be more accepting of others as well as ourselves. Too often, especially as we are bombarded by the false contemporary message of temporal importance, we feel inadequate and, thus, seek to present ourselves to others in ways that give them a false image. Grant us, as we break open the word this week, to be more atuned to what you have to say to us, whether that be in the word directly, or through the ideas of our brothers and sisters. May this opportunity to walk the road, continue to illuminate our minds and hearts to the beauty of the life you have given to us and help us to be more responsible in living as your children. Amen.

Additional prayers of the group

Lesson I: Exodus 20:1-17

And God spoke all these words, saying, "I am the Lord your God, who brought you out of the land of Egypt, out of the house of bondage. "You shall have no other gods before me. "You shall not make for yourself a graven image, or any likeness of anything that is in heaven above, or that is in the earth beneath, or that is in the water under the earth; you shall not bow down to them or serve them; for I the Lord your God am a jealous God, visiting the iniquity of the fathers upon the children to the third and the fourth generation of those who hate me, but showing steadfast love to thousands of those who love me and keep my commandments. "You shall not take the name of the Lord your God in vain; for the Lord will not hold him guiltless who takes his name in vain. "Remember the sabbath day, to keep it holy. Six days you shall labor, and do all your work; but the seventh day is a sabbath to the Lord your God; in it you shall not do any work, you, or your son, or your daughter, your manservant, or your maidservant, or your cattle, or the sojourner who is within your gates; for in six days the Lord made heaven and earth, the sea, and all that is in them, and rested the seventh day; therefore the Lord blessed the Sabbath day and hallowed it. "Honor your father and your mother, that your days may be long in the land which the Lord your God gives you. "You shall not kill. "You shall not commit adultery. "You shall not steal. "You shall not bear false witness against your neighbor. "You shall not covet your neighbor's house; you shall not covet your neighbor's wife, or his manservant, or his maidservant, or his ox, or his ass, or anything that is your neighbor's."

Lesson II: 1 Corinthians 1:18-25

For the word of the cross is folly to those who are perishing, but to us who are being saved it is the power of God. For it is written, "I will destroy the wisdom of the wise, and the cleverness of the clever I will thwart." Where is the wise man? Where is the scribe? Where is the debater of this age? Has not God made foolish the wisdom of the world? For since, in the wisdom of God, the world did not know God through wisdom, it pleased God through the folly of what we preach to save those who believe. For Jews demand signs and Greeks seek wisdom, but we preach Christ crucified, a stumbling block to Jews and folly to Gentiles, but to those who are called, both Jews and Greeks, Christ the power of God and the wisdom of God. For the foolishness of God is wiser than men, and the weakness of God is stronger than men.

Gospel: John 2:13-22

The Passover of the Jews was at hand, and Jesus went up to Jerusalem. In the temple he found those who were selling oxen and sheep and pigeons, and the money-changers at their business. And making a whip of cords, he drove them all, with the sheep and oxen, out of the temple; and he poured out the coins of the money-changers and overturned their tables. And he told those who sold the pigeons, "Take these things away; you shall not make my Father's house a house of trade." His disciples remembered that it was written, "Zeal for thy house will consume me." The Jews then said to him, "What sign have you to show us for doing this?" Jesus answered them, "Destroy this temple, and in three days I will raise it up." The Jews then said, "It has taken forty-six years to build this temple, and will you raise it up in three days?" But he spoke of the temple of his body. When therefore he was raised from the dead, his disciples remembered that he had said this; and they believed the scripture and the word which Jesus had spoken.

Reflection:
You Can't Fool God

A man lived in an old stone cottage that was badly in need of repair. He made do, day by day, and got on with his life, struggling to wrench a living from the meager land. But eventually the rain that leaked in on him got too heavy and the wind around his ears was too cold. He had to do something about the gap in his wall.

Up on the hillside there was an ancient Celtic cross. It had stood there since time immemorial. It was silent and uncomplaining in the Atlantic gales that swept over it, but its very silence said something about continuity, community, and interrelatedness. It had become a part of the local imagination and without ever really thinking about it, the people knew with a sound instinct, that is was very important. It had something to say about what they hoped to be. It had something to do with the coming of the kingdom.

The man from the cottage, who was a stonecutter, went up to the cross one dark night. One of those stone arcs, he thought, would fit exactly the hole in his wall. He would come the next day with a hammer and a chisel and remove it. He smiled, perhaps uneasily, as he thought of how much warmer his house would be without the perpetual drafts. Almost satisfied with his decision, he turned toward his homeward path, but his plans were rudely interrupted. In the distance he clearly saw flames rising from his cottage. Panic-stricken he ran across the rough field, but when he arrived home his cottage was still standing as he had left it. The fire had only been in his imagination.

A few days later, common sense again reasserted itself and he once again set off up the hill with his hammer and chisel. It was dark, but he looked about warily, lest anyone else should see him there. It was only a piece of stone after all, and he needed it. He started to chip. The sound of the hammer against the solid head of the chisel rang out through the night like the tolling of a bell to alarm the very heavens. But he continued to chip until he remembered the strange events of his previous attempt and looked over his shoulder nervously in the direction of his cottage. There, on the distant skyline, a fire raged. Again, he ran home in terror only to find his cottage unharmed, just as he had left it.

More cold nights came and went; sleep came uneasily to the stonecutter. The bizarre images of dream and nightmare entangled themselves among the pressing urgencies of everyday life. The fierce winds from the sea were stronger by far than the breezes that fluttered through his unease. He made up his mind that the very next day his cottage would be sound again and that no irrational fears would deflect him from his purpose.

He walked up the hill, without looking to the right or the left. He worked quickly and efficiently, closing the doors of his mind firmly against any distraction, real or imagined. Soon the stone arc was in his sack. This time there were no flames on the horizon and, thus, no flash of panic disturbed him. He turned his back on the mutilated cross and walked home through the quiet of the night. And when he arrived home the cottage was a heap of smoldering ashes.[9]

The stonecutter thought he could fool God, that no one would know what he was doing. But, even though he received many warnings, he continued and, in the end, disaster struck. Today, as our Lenten journey continues, our scripture readings focus on the law of God and God's knowledge of what we do. We have been given the proper path, a path that for many seems to be folly, but it is the one road that leads to life eternal.

In the book of Exodus, we read about how God in a formal way brought the law, one of the most central concepts of Judaism. Moses was given two stone tablets upon which God had written a plan for life, loving God and loving neighbor by paying respect to both in all that we do and say. The Decalogue was given by God to the Israelites as a means to free them from the past and to provide a clear path for the future. The Israelites knew the proper way, but they did not always follow it. We often find ourselves in the same predicament.

9   Taken from Margaret Silf. *Sacred Spaces: Stations on a Celtic Way* (Brewster, Massachusetts: Paraclete Press, 2001): pp 49-51.

Jesus, in the gospel again, shows the proper path. He forcefully removes the buyers and sellers from the temple, thereby showing all those present what God wanted. The temple was to be a house of prayer, not a marketplace for thieves. John goes on, however, to say something more emphatic — Jesus was well aware of what was in the human heart. Jesus knows our intentions; he knows what is going on. The Hebrews had the law; they knew what was right and proper. Yet, many chose another route; they thought they could fool God.

Lent is the perfect time to take an account of our lives and see where we stand in our relationship with God. We know the law perfectly well; we know what is right and what we should do. Yet, too often our personal desire, the allure of the world, and even societal pressures cause us to go astray. Often today the world sees what we value, that is the law of God, as rather foolish and possibly not applicable in the twenty-first century. Saint Paul, writing almost 2000 years ago, encountered the same situation and, thus, he wrote to the Corinthians that while the cross seems to be folly to some, it is the source of salvation for those who believe. God's folly is wiser than human wisdom and God's perceived weakness is greater than human strength.

We, too often, unfortunately, are like the stonecutter. Warnings of problems and consequences come our way and we choose to ignore them. We continue on the path of self-destruction, whether it is a health-related issue, situation at work, personal relationship, or family problem. The path that leads to life is clear, but we often choose another path. Jesus makes the choice very clear in the Sermon on the Mount: "Enter through the narrow gate, for the road to destruction is clear, the path is wide and many choose to follow it. But how narrow is the gate to life, how rough the road, and how few there are who find it" (Matthew 7:13-14).

Discussion Questions:

1. When was the last time I tried to "pull the wool over the eyes" of a family member, friend, or colleague at work?

2. In my relationships with others, do I try to make myself out to be more than I am, someone better or more perfect than is my reality?

3. When I look in the mirror, what do I see? Can I accept the person I am and believe, since we are made in the image and likeness of God, that I am indeed beautiful and important in God's sight?

4. Can I accept my faults and failings as part of the human condition; can I admit when I have made mistakes and not feel ashamed about my shortcomings?

5. Do I truly understand that there are consequences associated with the actions of my life? Can I fully acknowledge that there is no fooling God?

Concluding Prayer:

Loving God, our readings and discussion teach us that we must not try to put on airs, but rather to live in the presence of God as we are. Our society judges people and marks their value by the material wealth we possess, the power we hold, and the prestige which others give to us. These, while important to the world, are of no importance to you. Teach us today, as the scriptures describe, that we must be content with who we are and love ourselves as you, our creator, loved us into existence. Help us to accept our faults and failures, especially during this Lenten season, and see through our human incompleteness our absolute need for you and the redemption given to us by the sacrifice of your son, Jesus Christ. May we honor you by living in fidelity as the person you created, and not who the world says we ought to be. Help us to see the beauty of our lives and to celebrate who we are, children of God, and heirs of the promise of eternal life. Amen.

Lent 4

Theme: Follow The Light Who Is Christ

Opening Prayer:

God, our heavenly Father, our Creator and guide, we once again gather to break open and be nourished by your word and our discussions with our brothers and sisters. We come as we are, with our worries and concerns, thoughts of our jobs and our families, but with open hearts and minds to be fed in the most important of ways, through your word. As we gather together, help us to continue to be faithful as we walk this sacred journey of Lent. Having completed half of our journey, we look forward with eager anticipation to the possibilities and opportunities that will come our way, if we remain open to the many ways you come to us, through opportunities and challenges, various events, and most especially others who we meet along the road. May our time together be filled with many blessings as we continue to search for, and be enlightened by, the scriptures which guide our life each and every day. Amen.

Additional prayers of the group

Lesson I: Numbers 21:4-9

From Mount Hor they set out by the way to the Red Sea, to go around the land of Edom; and the people became impatient on the way. And the people spoke against God and against Moses, "Why have you brought us up out of Egypt to die in the wilderness? For there is no food and no water, and we loathe this worthless food." Then the Lord sent fiery serpents among the people, and they bit the people, so that many people of Israel died. And the people came to Moses, and said, "We have sinned, for we have spoken against the Lord and against you; pray to the Lord, that he take away the serpents from us." So Moses prayed for the people. And the Lord said to Moses, "Make a fiery serpent, and set it on a pole; and everyone who is bitten, when he sees it, shall live." So Moses made a bronze serpent, and set it on a pole; and if a serpent bit any man, he would look at the bronze serpent and live.

Lesson II: Ephesians 2:1-10

And you he made alive, when you were dead through the trespasses and sins in which you once walked, following the course of this world, following the prince of the power of the air, the spirit that is now at work in the sons of disobedience. Among these we all once lived in the passions of our flesh, following the desires of body and mind, and so we were by nature children of wrath, like the rest of mankind. But God, who is rich in mercy, out of the great love with which he loved us, even when we were dead through our trespasses, made us alive together with Christ (by grace you have been saved), and raised us up with him, and made us sit with him in the heavenly places in Christ Jesus, that in the coming ages he might show the immeasurable riches of his grace in kindness toward us in Christ Jesus. For by grace you have been saved through faith; and this is not your own doing, it is the gift of God — not because of works, lest any man should boast. For we are his workmanship, created in Christ Jesus for good works, which God prepared beforehand, that we should walk in them.

Gospel: John 3:14-21

And as Moses lifted up the serpent in the wilderness, so must the Son of man be lifted up, that whoever believes in him may have eternal life."For God so loved the world that he gave his only Son, that whoever believes in him should not perish but have eternal life. For God sent the Son into the world, not to condemn the world, but that the world might be saved through him. He who believes in him is not condemned; he who does not believe is condemned already, because he has not believed in the name of the only Son of God. And this is the judgment, that the light has come into the world, and men loved darkness rather than light, because their deeds were evil. For every one who does evil hates the light, and does not come to the light, lest his deeds should be exposed. But he who does what is true comes to the light, that it may be clearly seen that his deeds have been wrought in God.

Reflection:
Follow The Light Who Is Christ

A traveler was returning home from a distant land. At nightfall he arrived at the entrance of a vast forest, but because he did not know the region he asked a local shepherd for help. The shepherd replied, "The forest is filled with many large beasts, snakes, and there are many paths that lead to the Great Abyss." "What is the Great Abyss?" asked the traveler. "It is the abyss which surrounds the forest, but you need to be led in the proper way. I have stationed myself here at the entrance of the forest to assist and direct travelers should they wish my assistance. I have also placed my sons at different intervals to assist me in this good work. Their services and mine are at your disposal; we are ready to accompany you if you so desire."

The candor and venerable appearance of the old man satisfied the traveler, who accepted the proposal. The shepherd held a lantern with one hand, and in the other he grabbed the arm of the traveler. They set out on their journey to traverse the forest. After walking some distance, the traveler became quite weary, and thus the two stopped at the house of one of the shepherd's sons. At the shepherd's call, the door of the small cabin opened and the traveler and shepherd were escorted inside for warmth, food, and drink. Refreshed and somewhat rested, they again set out. In this same manner, the traveler journeyed with the shepherd for the rest of the night, stopping at different cabins built along the path, each inhabited by a son of the shepherd. With the dawning of the day, the traveler finally arrived on the other side of the forest, without incident. Only then did he appreciate the magnitude of the service rendered him by the shepherd and his sons, for at the very edge of the forest, right before his feet, lay a frightful precipice. "This," said the shepherd, "is the Great Abyss. No one knows its depth for it is always covered with a thick fog which no one can penetrate." The traveler seemed sad and shed a tear which prompted the shepherd to ask, "Are you sad?" "How can I be anything but sad knowing that so many people are swallowed up each day by the darkness of the abyss?" The shepherd had to agree, commenting, "In vain, too, my sons and I often offer our services. Many despise our advice; they choose to live in their own darkness. Yet, there is only one way to traverse the forest and that is with our assistance." The traveler again offered his gratitude and then walked away realizing that he would return to his own land. His family and friends were there to welcome him.

The traveler was wise enough to seek the assistance of the shepherd and his sons, to give him the light that was necessary to traverse the dangerous forest and to avoid certain death in the Great Abyss. In a similar way, our readings on this fourth Sunday of Lent tell us that we must follow the light and avoid the darkness that often pervades our lives, confident that with the light we will find the eternal life we seek. The light will always come to us, but we may or may not follow. This choice is, of course, our free will. It is the existential choice of saying yes or no to God.

In the first lesson from the book of Numbers we hear about the Hebrews and their inability to follow the law of God. Constantly complaining against Moses, who had been assigned by God to lead them to the promised land, they, like the unnamed travelers in the story who refused to take the assistance of the man and his sons, found themselves in dire straits. They did not fall into the abyss, but rather into death through the snakes that were sent to harass them. Like the man in the story, Moses provided the antidote by mounting the bronze serpent on a pole. Rather than following the light of Moses, the Israelites followed a different route, until, through the action of God, they came back to their senses. But it took the death of many members of the community before they got the message. Moses was the guiding light, but it was necessary for the Israelites to follow.

In the gospel, we again hear about the light. John says the light came into the world, not to condemn but to save all people. Unfortunately, the Jews of Jesus' day, like their ancient Hebrew ancestors, did not pay attention to the light. As with the prophets, Jesus came to give warmth, to renew strength, to give hope. Jesus came to give direction to a world which was moving toward ruin. Despite all the possibilities that Jesus provided, John says that the people preferred darkness. The light exposed the deeds of the people and these deeds were wicked. The people said "no" to the light; they chose the darkness. The people with their decision lost their direction and consequently found themselves in coldness and despair.

The message of scripture must be applied to our own lives. We absolutely need Jesus: his warmth, his strength, his comfort, his direction. As Saint Paul says in today's second lesson, it is through Christ that we have been brought back to life from the darkness of sin. It is through the light of Christ that salvation is ours through faith. We, through our ability to choose, can say yes or no to God. We must say "yes" to God; we must seek the light. The person who welcomes the light avoids condemnation. The one who welcomes the light finds eternal life. Thus, we must welcome the light and, possibly more importantly, cast out the darkness, from our personal lives and that of society.

The holy season of Lent is a perfect time to reflect upon casting out the darkness from our personal lives. It might be a bad habit, some routine that we know gets us in trouble or drives us away from God. It may be some vice, excessive drinking, smoking, drugs, or illicit sex, that is the darkness of our life. We need to cast it out. But we also need to cast out the darkness of society. What have we done lately to cast out the darkness of ignorance in our world? What have we done to cast out the darkness of arrogance? What can we do to cast out the darkness of poverty which is too rampant in our first-world comfortable society? How can we help to cast out the darkness of violence, against individuals, groups or society? We might not be able to make systemic change on our own, but working together as a community we can do great things. But we must make the initial effort. Think globally, but act locally!

Each day is an opportunity to rediscover the light. As the gospel says, "God so loved the world that he gave his only Son, that whoever believes in him may not die but may have eternal life" (John 3:16). God sent the Son, the light, so that we could return to the place of our origin with God. Let us seek the light; let us welcome the Lord. Let us say "yes" to God's call in our life and in this way find eternal salvation as well.

Discussion Questions:

1. What manifestations of darkness pervade my life? What darkness needs to be cast out and replaced with the light of Christ?

2. Does the darkness present in the world discourage me from shining the light? Do I have the courage of my convictions?

3. What can I do to bring more light to our often dark and foreboding world?

4. When the darkness of defeat or major problems come my way, what has been my reaction? Can I rise up and continue my search for the light that is Christ?

5. What can I do to dispel the darkness and bring the light to one who lives in the shadows or depths of despair?

Concluding Prayer:

Good and gracious God, the light of your son, Jesus Christ, is a beacon of hope for all in our contemporary world which is so often darkened by sin. We have taken the time and made the effort to reflect upon the manifestations of darkness in our world, both personally and in society so that we can move in a more positive direction and bring our community back to the reality of our absolute need for you. While the manifestations of darkness are varied and multiple, we know that the light which Jesus can bring can dispel the deepest darkness and the greatest despair. May we learn from the scriptures and confidently believe that you are with us every step of the way, enjoying with us the height of every triumph and holding us close during the depth of every defeat. Help us to understand and manifest in our lives the knowledge that without you nothing is possible, but with you all things are possible. Let the light of your son, Jesus, shine upon us, and bring us to greater wholeness in all we say and do. Amen.

Lent 5
Theme: Dying To New Life

Opening Prayer:

Good and gracious God, it is good that we are here. Our journey of Lent has traversed much ground and we have gained significantly in the process by studying and discussing your word. Once again we take time from our busy schedules to pause, put aside the day-to day routine, our worries and anxieties, and seek to center on you, your word, and how we can become more enlightened so as to walk more faithfully the road that leads back home to you. Help us as we gather this week to enter even more fully and with greater fidelity into the challenges your word provides for us. Life often throws us many challenges, hurdles, and obstacles; we do not need to seek them, for they will find us. However, we do welcome the challenge you bring to us in scripture, including the need to concentrate less on ourselves and more on the needs of the common good. May our time together bring many graces, help us to grow in holiness, and aid us to better serve our brothers and sisters. Amen.

Additional prayers of the group

Lesson I: Jeremiah 31:31-34

"Behold, the days are coming, says the Lord, when I will make a new covenant with the house of Israel and the house of Judah, not like the covenant which I made with their fathers when I took them by the hand to bring them out of the land of Egypt, my covenant which they broke, though I was their husband, says the Lord. But this is the covenant which I will make with the house of Israel after those days, says the Lord: I will put my law within them, and I will write it upon their hearts; and I will be their God, and they shall be my people. And no longer shall each man teach his neighbor and each his brother, saying, 'Know the Lord,' for they shall all know me, from the least of them to the greatest, says the Lord; for I will forgive their iniquity, and I will remember their sin no more."

Lesson II: Hebrews 5:5-10

So also Christ did not exalt himself to be made a high priest, but was appointed by him who said to him, "Thou art my Son, today I have begotten thee"; as he says also in another place, "Thou art a priest forever, after the order of Melchizedek." In the days of his flesh, Jesus offered up prayers and supplications, with loud cries and tears, to him who was able to save him from death, and he was heard for his godly fear. Although he was a Son, he learned obedience through what he suffered; and being made perfect he became the source of eternal salvation to all who obey him, being designated by God a high priest after the order of Melchizedek.

Gospel: John 12:20-33

Now among those who went up to worship at the feast were some Greeks. So these came to Philip, who was from Bethsaida in Galilee, and said to him, "Sir, we wish to see Jesus." Philip went and told Andrew; Andrew went with Philip and they told Jesus. And Jesus answered them, "The hour has come for the son of man to be glorified. Truly, truly, I say to you, unless a grain of wheat falls into the earth and dies, it remains alone; but if it dies, it bears much fruit. He who loves his life loses it, and he who hates his life in this world will keep it for eternal life. If any one serves me, he must follow me; and where I am, there shall my servant be also; if any one serves me, the Father will honor him.

"Now is my soul troubled. And what shall I say? 'Father, save me from this hour'? No, for this purpose I have come to this hour. Father, glorify thy name." Then a voice came from heaven, "I have glorified it, and I will glorify it again." The crowd standing by heard it and said that it had thundered. Others said, "An angel has spoken to him." Jesus answered, "This voice has come for your sake, not for mine. Now is the judgment of this world, now shall the ruler of this world be cast out; and I, when I am lifted up from the earth, will draw all men to myself." He said this to show by what death he was to die.

Reflection:
Dying To New Life

If you look up the word paradox in the dictionary, you will find a definition that runs something like this: a statement which on first examination appears to be false, but on a closer reading is found to be true. There are many examples of paradoxes. We can look at two varied ones — one from literature and one from the world of mathematics.

In the famous dialogue "Meno" by Plato, Socrates and his friend Meno are in a deep discussion. Meno poses the following question, "Is it possible to know that which one has not learned?" Meno immediately answers his own question saying, *no*; there is nothing that a human knows that has not been previously learned. Socrates, however, looks at this question, known as "Meno's Paradox," and says, *yes*. He asks, "Did you learn how to breathe?" He continues, "Did you learn how to love another person?" To both questions, Meno responds, "No." Thus, there are certain things that are so innate to the human person that one knows them without learning.

The second paradox is from the world of mathematics. If you want to go from point A to point B and you move exactly one-half of the remaining distance between the two points on each move, you will never arrive at your destination. At first glance you might say, that certainly cannot be correct; I must be able to figure this out. The statement is a paradox. If you can move only half the remaining distance each time, you will come close, infinitesimally close, but you will never arrive.

Although we can all probably think of many other paradoxes, we might ask, "What is the greatest of all paradoxes?" The answer most assuredly is Christianity. Christ himself is a paradox. Jesus is God, yet he is human at the same time. How is this possible? It is a mystery, yet it is the truth; it is a paradox. Most especially, the teaching of Jesus, his message which forms the basis of our faith, is a paradox. In today's gospel, Jesus gives us the classic Christian paradox, "Unless the grain of wheat falls to the earth and dies, it remains just a grain of wheat — but if it dies, then it produces much fruit." Again Jesus says the same thing in different words: "The person who loves his life, loses it, while the one who hates his life in this world preserves it to life eternal."

How is this possible? It cannot be true, we say, but it is. It is a paradox. Yes, the reality is that Jesus' statement is true. What is more important is to ask, what does it mean for us? Do we need to die to find eternal life? Is our life here without merit? Are our efforts each day useless? The meaning and significance of Jesus' statement, this ultimate paradox, is that we are to give our lives for others. This is done through sacrifice. We are to give to others. We are to take less so that others may have more. It is done by sharing what we have in material things. In short, as the expression goes, it is to live simply so others may simply live.

How do we do this; how do we live for others? The principal way that Jesus' life suggests is through service. We are to serve those who are meek and lowly, those who seem to count for little in our world. It is ministry and service to the poor and homeless. Our ultimate goal should be to die in Christ and rise to a new, fuller, and eternal life. But this does not mean that we are not accountable now. The Christian paradox is not only for our time of death, it must be lived each day in our relationship with God and God's people.

How can we live this Christian paradox? The first two readings provide some insight. First, we learn that we must renew our relationship with God and God's people. As Jeremiah told the Hebrews that God was making a new covenant with them, a covenant not on tablets of stone but written on their hearts, so must we build a renewed relationship with God. Next, we must learn as did Jesus that obedience, the ability to follow God's paradoxical plan, is found through suffering. That is what we are told in the second reading. Christ has given us a new way of life, a way which finds its direction by renunciation of self, sacrifice, and service.

Jesus says in the gospel that his hour has come. Our hour has come as well. It is our hour for action; it is our hour to renew our relationship with God. We must be the paradox that our Christian faith demands of us. The world is fascinated with power, wealth and prestige; we must offer an alternative. When the world seeks power, we must choose humility. When society seeks wealth, we must choose voluntary poverty. When the world seeks prestige, we must seek to freely associate with the lowly of society. Dying to the world produces nothing, but dying to self in this world produces many wonderful gifts such as renunciation, sacrifice, and service. In short, dying to self produces the gifts which lead us to a fuller relationship with God and God's people.

Yes, it is true, Christianity is a paradox. Our life finds its greatest merit through death. Physical death, when God calls us to himself, will bring us to the presence of God and eternal life. But more importantly, dying to self now produces much fruit for God's people, and the kingdom of God is made more manifest each day. Therefore, let us sacrifice; let us be of service to others. Let us die to self, as the Christian paradox calls us to do, and in the process find eternal life as well!

Discussion Questions:

1. Can I place my full trust in Jesus' paradoxical statement that we only find life through death?

2. How do I understand and more importantly manifest Jesus' challenge to "die for others"?

3. How have others been willing to die for me, to go out of their way and sacrifice themselves so that I might have more and draw closer to God?

4. How can I teach, by word and action, the necessity to lower ourselves for the benefit of others, knowing that in the end we will benefit?

5. In a world that exalts the individual, what can I do to promote the common good at work, in my community, in the church?

Concluding Prayer:

Lord Jesus, your whole life was a great manifestation of the message in our readings. You came as an innocent child and willingly suffered and died for all of us, unworthy though we are. This season we celebrate and the specific scriptures we have studied this week must prompt us to consider our response to the sacrifices you made for us. Help us, O Lord, to be more grateful for what you have done for us by passing along the benefits we have received from your sacrifice to others. Help us to be generous in giving of our time, talent, and treasure, to sacrifice ourselves somewhat so that others may enjoy, to some small extent, the day-to-day privileges that are the norm for us. May we see the benefit in our sacrifice, not only by the material assistance that others may receive, but more importantly by the spiritual benefits that we will gain. For by imitating you, and living your gospel message, we will certainly draw closer to you, the source of all that we are, have, and hope to be. Amen.

Palm Sunday / Passion Sunday
Theme: The Paradox Of Death

Opening Prayer:

Good and gracious God, as we enter Holy Week, this sacred time when we walk the road of your son, Jesus, from triumph, to crucifixion and ultimately to resurrection, we ask for your special blessing. While the world continues to move at lightning speed to achieve all the apparent necessities of life, we, the Christian community, must slow down so as to be able to walk more closely and faithfully this important journey. As we enter into this special week of prayer, we ask you to calm our hearts, enlighten our minds, and cleanse our souls so that we may be adequately and properly prepared for the trek we undertake. We begin this journey in triumph, standing with the crowd and crying, "Hosanna." Too often, however, we also know that we follow the crowd that ultimately shouts, "Crucify him!" Help us to not follow that crowd, but rather to follow in the footsteps of Jesus, seen in his sacrificial acts of love as the one and only way that leads us home to you. Amen.

Additional prayers of the group

Lesson I: Isaiah 50:4-9a

The Lord God has given me the tongue of those who have taught, that I may know how to sustain with a word him that is weary. Morning by morning he wakens, he wakens my ear to hear as those who are taught. The Lord God has opened my ear, and I was not rebellious, I turned not backward. I gave my back to the smiters, and my cheeks to those who pulled out the beard; I hid not my face from shame and spitting. For the Lord God helps me; therefore I have not been confounded; therefore I have set my face like a flint, and I know that I shall not be put to shame; he who vindicates me is near. Who will contend with me? Let us stand up together. Who is my adversary? Let him come near to me. Behold, the Lord God helps me; who will declare me guilty? Behold, all of them will wear out like a garment; the moth will eat them up.

Lesson II: Philippians 2:5-11

Have this mind among yourselves, which is yours in Christ Jesus, who, though he was in the form of God, did not count equality with God a thing to be grasped, but emptied himself, taking the form of a servant, being born in the likeness of men. And being found in human form he humbled himself and became obedient unto death, even death on a cross. Therefore God has highly exalted him and bestowed on him the name which is above every name, that at the name of Jesus every knee should bow, in heaven and on earth and under the earth, and every tongue confess that Jesus Christ is Lord, to the glory of God the Father.

Gospel: Mark 14:1-15:47 (or Mark 15:1-39 [40-47])

It was now two days before the Passover and the feast of Unleavened Bread. And the chief priests and the scribes were seeking how to arrest him by stealth, and kill him; for they said, "Not during the feast, lest there be a tumult of the people."

And while he was at Bethany in the house of Simon the leper, as he sat at table, a woman came with an alabaster flask of ointment of pure nard, very costly, and she broke the flask and poured it over his head. But there were some who said to themselves indignantly, "Why was the ointment thus wasted? For this ointment might have been sold for more than three hundred denarii, and given to the poor." And they reproached her. But Jesus said, "Let her alone; why do you trouble her? She has done a beautiful thing to me. For you always have the poor with you, and whenever you will, you can do good to them; but you will not always have me. She has done what she could; she has anointed my body beforehand for burying. And truly, I say to you, wherever the gospel is preached in the whole world, what she has done will be told in memory of her."

Then Judas Iscariot, who was one of the twelve, went to the chief priests in order to betray him to them. And when they heard it they were glad, and promised to give him money. And he sought an opportunity to betray him.

And on the first day of feast, when they sacrificed the Passover lamb, his disciples said to him, "Where will you have us go and prepare for you to eat the Passover?" And he sent two of his disciples, and said to them, "Go into the city, and a man carrying a jar of water will meet you; follow him, and wherever he enters, say to the householder, 'The Teacher says, Where is my guest room, where I am to eat the Passover with my disciples?' And he will show you a large upper room furnished and ready; there prepare for us." And the disciples set out and went to the city, and found it as he had told them; and they prepared the passover. And when it was evening he came with the twelve. And as they were at table eating, Jesus said, "Truly, I say to you, one of you will betray me, one who is eating with me." They began to be sorrowful, and to say to him one after another, "Is it I?" He said to them, "It is one of the twelve, one who is dipping bread into the dish with me. For the son of man goes as it is written of him, but woe to that man by whom the son of man is betrayed! It would have been better for that man if he had not been born."

And as they were eating, he took bread, and blessed, and broke it, and gave it to them, and said, "Take; this is my body." And he took a cup, and when he had given thanks he gave it to them, and they all drank of it. And he said to them, "This is my blood of the covenant, which is poured out for many. Truly, I say to you, I shall not drink again of the fruit of the vine until that day when I drink it new in the kingdom of God."

And when they had sung a hymn, they went out to the Mount of Olives. And Jesus said to them, "You will all fall away; for it is written, 'I will strike the shepherd, and the sheep will be scattered.' But after I am raised up, I will go before you to Galilee." Peter said to him, "Even though they all fall away, I will not." And Jesus said to him, "Truly, I say to you, this very night, before the cock crows twice, you will deny me three times." But he said vehemently, "If I must die with you, I will not deny you." And they all said the same.

And they went to a place which was called Gethsemane; and he said to his disciples, "Sit here, while I pray." And he took with him Peter and James and John, and began to be greatly distressed and troubled. And he said to them, "My soul is very sorrowful, even to death; remain here, and watch." And going a little farther, he fell on the ground and prayed that, if it were possible, the hour might pass from him. And he said, "Abba, Father, all things are possible to thee; remove this cup from me; yet not what I will, but what thou wilt." And he came and found them sleeping, and he said to Peter, "Simon, are you asleep? Could you not watch one hour? Watch and pray that you may not enter into temptation; the spirit indeed is willing, but the flesh is weak." And again he went away and prayed, saying the same words. And again he came and found them sleeping, for their eyes were very heavy; and they did not know what to answer him. And he came the third time, and said to them, "Are you still sleeping and taking your rest? It is enough; the hour has come; the son of man is betrayed into the hands of sinners. Rise, let us be going; see, my betrayer is at hand."

And immediately, while he was still speaking, Judas came, one of the twelve, and with him a crowd with swords and clubs, from the chief priests and the scribes and the elders. Now the betrayer had given them a sign, saying, "The one I shall kiss is the man; seize him and lead him away under guard." And when he came, he went up to him at once, and said, "Master!" And he kissed him. And they laid hands on him and seized him. But one of those who stood by drew his sword, and struck the slave of the high priest and cut off his ear. And Jesus said to them, "Have you come out as against a robber, with swords and clubs to capture me? Day after day I was with you in the temple teaching, and you did not seize me. But let the scriptures be fulfilled." And they all forsook him, and fled. And a young man followed him, with nothing but a linen cloth about his body; and they seized him, but he left the linen cloth and ran away naked.

And they led Jesus to the high priest; and all the chief priests and the elders and the scribes were assembled. And Peter had followed him at a distance, right into the courtyard of the high priest; and he was sitting with the guards, and warming himself at the fire. Now the chief priests and the whole council sought testimony against Jesus to put him to death; but they found none. For many bore false witness against him, and their witness did not agree. And some stood up and bore false witness against him, saying, "We heard him say, 'I will destroy this temple that is made with hands, and in three days I will build another, not made with hands.'" Yet not even so did their testimony agree. And the high priest stood up in the midst, and asked Jesus, "Have you no answer to make? What is it that these men testify against you?" But he was silent and made no answer. Again the high priest asked him, "Are you the Christ, the Son of the Blessed?" And Jesus said, "I am; and you will see the Son of man seated at the right hand of Power, and coming with the clouds of heaven." And the high priest tore his garments, and said, "Why do we still need witnesses? You have heard his blasphemy. What is your decision?" And they all condemned him as deserving death. And some began to spit on him, and to cover his face, and to strike him, saying to him, "Prophesy!" And the guards received him with blows.

And as Peter was below in the courtyard, one of the maids of the high priest came; and seeing Peter warming himself, she looked at him, and said, "You also were with the Nazarene, Jesus." But he denied it, saying, "I neither know nor understand what you mean." And he went out into the gateway. And the maid saw him, and began again to say to the bystanders, "This man is one of them." But again he denied it. And after a little while again the bystanders said to Peter, "Certainly you are one of them; for you are a Galilean." But he began to invoke a curse on himself and to swear, "I do not know this man of whom you speak." And immediately the cock crowed a second time. And Peter remembered how Jesus had said to him, "Before the cock crows twice, you will deny me three times." And he broke down and wept.

And as soon as it was morning the chief priests, with the elders and scribes, and the whole council held a consultation; and they bound Jesus and led him away and delivered him to Pilate. And Pilate asked him, "Are you the King of the Jews?" And he answered him, "You have said so." And the chief priests accused him of many things. And Pilate again asked him, "Have you no answer to make? See how many charges they bring against you." But Jesus made no further answer, so that Pilate wondered.

Now at the feast he used to release for them one prisoner for whom they asked. And among the rebels in prison, who had committed murder in the insurrection, there was a man called Barabbas. And the crowd came up and began to ask Pilate to do as he was wont to do for them. And he answered them, "Do you want me to release for you the King of the Jews?" For he perceived that it was out of envy that the chief priests had delivered him up. But the chief priests stirred up the crowd to have him release for them Barabbas instead. And Pilate again said to them, "Then what shall I do with the man whom you call the King of the Jews?" And they cried out again, "Crucify him!" And Pilate said to them, "Why, what evil has he done?" But they shouted all the more, "Crucify him!" So Pilate, wishing to satisfy the crowd, released for them Barabbas; and having scourged Jesus, he delivered him to be crucified.

And the soldiers led him away inside the palace (that is, the praetorium); and they called together the whole battalion. And they clothed him in a purple cloak, and plaiting a crown of thorns they put it on him. And they began to salute him, "Hail, King of the Jews!" And they struck his head with a reed, and spat upon him, and they knelt down in homage to him. And when they had mocked him, they stripped him of the purple cloak, and put his own clothes on him. And they led him out to crucify him.

And they compelled a passer-by, Simon of Cyrene, who was coming in from the country, the father of Alexander and Rufus, to carry his cross. And they brought him to the place called Golgotha (which means the place of a skull). And they offered him wine mingled with myrrh; but he did not take it. And they crucified him, and divided his garments among them, casting lots for them, to decide what each should take. And it was the third hour, when they crucified him. And the inscription of the charge against him read, "The King of the Jews." And with him they crucified two robbers, one on his right and one on his left. And those who passed by derided him, wagging their heads, and saying, "Aha! You who would destroy the temple and build it in three days, save yourself, and come down from the cross!" So also the chief priests mocked him to one another with the scribes, saying, "He saved others; he cannot save himself. Let the Christ, the King of Israel, come down now from the cross, that we may see and believe." Those who were crucified with him also reviled him.

And when the sixth hour had come, there was darkness over the whole land until the ninth hour. And at the ninth hour Jesus cried with a loud voice, "Eloi, Eloi, lama sabach-thani?" which means, "My God, my God, why hast thou forsaken me?" And some of the bystanders hearing it said, "Behold, he is calling Elijah." And one ran and, filling a sponge full of vinegar, put it on a reed and gave it to him to drink, saying, "Wait, let us see whether Elijah will come to take him down." And Jesus uttered a loud cry, and breathed his last. And the curtain of the temple was torn in two, from top to bottom. And when the centurion, who stood facing him, saw that he thus breathed his last, he said, "Truly this man was the Son of God!" There were also women looking on from afar, among whom were Mary Magdalene, and Mary the mother of James the younger and of Joses, and Salome, who, when he was in Galilee, followed him, and ministered to him; and also many other women who came up with him to Jerusalem.

And when evening had come, since it was the day of Preparation, that is, the day before the sabbath, Joseph of Arimathea, a respected member of the council, who was also himself looking for the kingdom of God, took courage and went to Pilate, and asked for the body of Jesus. And Pilate wondered if he were already dead; and summoning the centurion, he asked him whether he was already dead. And when he learned from the centurion that he was dead, he granted the body to Joseph. And he bought a linen shroud, and taking him down, wrapped him in the linen shroud, and laid him in a tomb which had been hewn out of the rock; and he rolled a stone against the door of the tomb. Mary Magdalene and Mary the mother of Jesus saw where he was laid.

Reflection:
The Paradox Of Death

The motion picture *Patton*, produced in 1970, won eight Academy Awards, including one for George C. Scott as best actor, in his portrayal of the famous American World War II general. The film opens in a rather odd manner. Patton, in full military regalia, stands atop a platform; he is addressing his troops before they enter battle. In the course of his comments he states, "Some people say it is glorious to die for your country. But I say that the objective of war is to make the other guy die for his country." That simple statement says something very profound about what we as a society think of death. We see it as something that is to be shunned and avoided; it is dishonorable to die. Certainly anyone in a normal situation wants to live and desires that all friends and loved ones remain healthy and active. Still, for the Christian, one's attitude toward death must be different. We have been given life by God for the ultimate purpose to return to our Creator. We are on a journey which leads to God, but we can only arrive at the final destination through death.

Lent is a journey which in many ways simulates our whole life path, from birth to death. We began this season on Ash Wednesday when we received the sign of ashes, which not only speaks of our mortality but also of the journey that we entered. During this season, we have gone to the desert with Jesus to be tested by Satan with the great temptations which have haunted humans for ages — power, wealth, and prestige. We next went to a high mountain, with Jesus, Peter, James, and John, and we saw the Lord transfigured. It was a momentary external transformation, but what did that miraculous event in Jesus' life do to transform us on the inside? We have walked beside Jesus in the heat of the day and the cool of the evening, experiencing along the way his triumphs and his difficulties. Now we enter the final part of the journey, a road that leads to death, but also to resurrection and eternal life.

Holy Week is a remembrance of a series of events of which our readings speak today. Jesus is welcomed with hosannas and palms as the great king as he enters the great city of Jerusalem.

Yet, we already know the end of the story. In five days he will be crucified, but he will rise again! The mystery of the Easter Triduum, the principle which is so basic to Christianity yet was totally absent from Patton's speech, is that something wonderful can be created from the tragedy of death. Jesus is the suffering servant of the prophet Isaiah. He was the one who was prophesied to be abused and mocked by others, rejected, and spurned. Jesus is also the God-man in the famous Christological hymn of Saint Paul in his letter to the Philippians — the one who, although God, emptied himself of his divinity to take human form and experience death on a cross. Yes, it is this suffering servant, this God-man, who enters Jerusalem in triumph. It is this same one who eats dinner with his disciples and then willingly chooses death for the freedom and salvation of sinful humanity. He was an innocent victim of the hatred of human beings. Yet, it will be this same Jesus who will rise and bring all people for all time the possibility of salvation.

Jesus' journey to death and resurrection must give us hope. It is a hope, born in difficulty, which says, despite the paradox, that life can only come from death. If we are willing to continue the Lenten journey with Jesus to the end — if we will walk with him —- then we too will find good through evil, triumph through defeat, and life through death. Let us, therefore, continue our walk with Jesus; let us stay close to him and in the process find life without end!

Discussion Questions:

1. Saint Paul says that Jesus took on the condition of a slave. If I am to follow Jesus, what does this mean for me?

2. Am I truly afraid of death or can I, with the eyes of faith, see it as the ultimate opportunity to live in the presence of God?

3. Do I run from the challenges that force me to change gears or move in another direction in life, or can I willingly accept them and gain new experiences as a result?

4. Am I too comfortable in my steady state, unchanging life? What do I need to continue to move forward in my relationship with Christ?

5. Am I willing to suffer abuse, rejection, and being set aside by others as a result of my faith in Jesus? How far am I willing to go to profess what I believe?

Concluding Prayer:

O Lord, our God, we have begun this sacred journey of Holy Week. As we have heard and discussed the great sacrifice that your son, Jesus, endured for us, help us to be mindful of our need to be more cognizant of the needs of those around us. Grant us the grace to walk this road with grace and fidelity, and as we journey, to be observant of the needs of those around us. Jesus sacrificed himself willingly for all of us, unworthy as we are. His action must prompt us to consider our response to the situation of our life and most especially those whom we encounter along the journey. We ask you to help us to be more faithful to you by being more strident in our attempts to assist others. Give us the insight we need to be more open and charitable with our time, talent, and treasure, so that this Holy Week will be a blessed time and we can recommit ourselves more fully to be true disciples of Jesus, your son, and our brother, friend, and Lord. Amen.

Easter Sunday
Theme: The Amazement Of The Resurrection

Opening Prayer:

God our loving Father, your Son Jesus' triumph over death, brings joy to all as well as many possibilities. As we come together to contemplate, study, and discuss the resurrection and its meaning for us today, help us to realize the possibilities that exist before us. All of us, in different ways, have experienced forms of death in our life, whether it was the physical loss of someone close, the destruction of a relationship, financial ruin, or the estrangement of a loved one. Help us to see, through the power of Jesus' resurrection, that new life is possible for us as well. There is no need to wait until we return home to you to experience the power of the resurrection in our life. As we conclude this special time of Lent and close Holy Week with the greatest of all Christian celebrations, let us be filled with the grace and peace which only you can give. May we, as we conclude our journey, be filled with the same love that Jesus has for us, so that we can be more Christlike in all we say and do. Amen.

Additional prayers of the group

Lesson I: Isaiah 25:6-9

On this mountain the Lord of hosts will make for all peoples a feast of fat things, a feast of wine on the lees, of fat things full of marrow, of wine on the lees well refined. And he will destroy on this mountain the covering that is cast over all peoples, the veil that is spread over all nations. He will swallow up death for ever, and the Lord God will wipe away tears from all faces, and the reproach of his people he will take away from all the earth; for the Lord has spoken. It will be said on that day, "Lo, this is our God; we have waited for him, that he might save us. This is the Lord; we have waited for him; let us be glad and rejoice in his salvation."

Lesson II: 1 Corinthians 15:1-11

Now I would remind you, brethren, in what terms I preached to you the gospel, which you received, in which you stand, by which you are saved, if you hold it fast — unless you believed in vain. For I delivered to you as of first importance what I also received, that Christ died for our sins in accordance with the scriptures, that he was buried, that he was raised on the third day in accordance with the scriptures, and that he appeared to Cephas, then to the twelve. Then he appeared to more than five hundred brethren at one time, most of whom are still alive, though some have fallen asleep. Then he appeared to James, then to all the apostles. Last of all, as to one untimely born, he appeared also to me. For I am the least of the apostles, unfit to be called an apostle, because I persecuted the church of God. But by the grace of God I am what I am, and his grace toward me was not in vain. On the contrary, I worked harder than any of them, though it was not I, but the grace of God which is with me. Whether then it was I or they, so we preach and so you believed.

Gospel: Mark 16:1-8

And when the sabbath was past, Mary Magdalene, and Mary the mother of James, and Salome, bought spices, so that they might go and anoint him. And very early on the first day of the week they went to the tomb when the sun had risen. And they were saying to one another, "Who will roll away the stone for us from the door of the tomb?" And looking up, they saw that the stone was rolled back—it was very large. And entering the tomb, they saw a young man sitting on the right side, dressed in a white robe; and they were amazed. And he said to them, "Do not be amazed; you seek Jesus of Nazareth, who was crucified. He has risen, he is not here; see the place where they laid him. But go, tell his disciples and Peter that he is going before you to Galilee; there you will see him, as he told you." [8] And they went out and fled from the tomb; for trembling and astonishment had come upon them; and they said nothing to any one, for they were afraid.

Reflection:
The Amazement Of The Resurrection

"And they were amazed." These powerful words come from today's gospel. What do they tell us about the Easter message? These words suggest that the amazement that the disciples experienced at the sight of the empty tomb must be what we seek in our life. We do not need to wait until the Lord calls us to experience the power of the resurrection. Its power is here now, if we can only perceive it.

Hermann Hesse in his wonderful novel *Siddhartha* spoke in a very profound way how we can find the amazing power of the resurrection present in our world today. Siddhartha was the son of a Brahmin or religious holy man in the East. One day he went to his father and asked permission to leave the village of his birth in search of amazement and meaning in his life. Initially his father was hesitant to let him go, but the boy pressed his father and, thus, the older man allowed his son to leave. Siddhartha and his best friend gathered a few belongings and left the village the next day to seek amazement and meaning in life.

As the boys began their journey, they had traveled less than a day's walk from the village when they came upon a vast and wide river. Siddhartha looked upon the water and realized the emptiness which lay before him. Certainly anything amazing and meaningful cannot be found here; the river is vast but so empty. Their quest unfulfilled, the two boys hired a ferryman to take them to the other shore so they could continue their search.

After a few days of travel they came upon a group of ascetics, people who spend much time in prayer and reflection. Possibly, thought Siddhartha, the amazement and meaning of life he sought could be found here. The boys asked permission from the community leader to join the group and learn the ways of prayer and meditation. The boys stayed for several years growing from youths to young adults. But after learning the ways of prayer and filling himself with methods of reflection Siddhartha realized that the meaning of life was not to be found here either. Thus, the two friends moved on again.

After a few more days of travel they came upon a guru or holy man. They attached themselves to those who followed this man. After a short while, however, Siddhartha knew that this life was not amazing to him and thus not meaningful. His friend, however, found fulfillment, and thus, the two best friends parted company forever.

Siddhartha moved on in his quest to find amazement and the meaning of life and entered a great city. There he found work, love, and marriage. He lived and worked in the city for many years; he raised a family. Young adulthood turned to maturity and then to old age. Yet, although he had spent the vast majority of his life in the great city, he still had not found the amazement in life he had always sought.

Thus, as an old man, Siddhartha continued his search. He left the city and began to walk. The journey was long and tiring but he eventually came upon a river. It was the same river that he and his best friend had crossed so many years ago, when they first left their home village. The river was still wide and vast; it was still empty. But Siddhartha looked at the river with new eyes. He realized that he had spent his whole life trying to find amazement and the meaning of life by filling himself up. As an old man, he came to the knowledge that all that he had sought had been before him, wherever he was, all along. He only needed to empty himself enough in order to see it.

Why were Jesus' disciples amazed that first Easter morning? They saw that the tomb was empty and realized that their lives were full, cluttered with many things. The question for them was--could they empty themselves enough to receive God, the risen Lord?

We need to ask ourselves the same question. Can we be amazed at the power and presence of Christ in our world? God has been bringing and continues to bring new life to our world. The prophet Isaiah today speaks of a banquet that God prepares for us. Jesus was the one who, Isaiah said, "will swallow up death," which he indeed did. Interestingly, the first chronological account of Jesus' swallowing death, the resurrection, is not found in the gospels, but rather in 1 Corinthians as Saint Paul wrote this letter some ten to fifteen years before any of the evangelists. Paul told us that he hands to his readers what was "of first importance," that Jesus died and was resurrected. Indeed, without Jesus' death and especially his resurrection our faith is useless. Thus, we can understand why the disciples were amazed. But as Hermann Hesse's story indicates, the amazement does not need to be found "out there" but must be found within ourselves. We can make the resurrection meaningful today; all we have to do is look inside and find the answer.

We might not feel comfortable looking inside and just being. It is difficult to accept the moment. However, if we find the space for Christ in our hearts, then the amazement that was the disciples, the amazement that was the revelation of Siddhartha will be ours as well. Thus, let us on this Easter day, empty ourselves somewhat and replace that void with the amazement that only the resurrection of Jesus can bring.

Jesus' resurrection asks us to revive the human spirit deep down inside each one of us. The empty tomb encourages us to be empty enough to be filled with God. Let us today be resurrected; let us be amazed, today and to life eternal!

Discussion Questions:

1. What do I need to clean out from my life in order to find sufficient room for the resurrected Lord?

2. In the busyness of daily life, can I find sufficient time each and every day for prayer and reflection?

3. Jesus' resurrection brings new life. What needs to be resurrected, reoriented, or redirected in my life?

4. How do I utilize my time? Do I fill it with all of the pleasures of the world or does God have an integral place in my day-to-day activity?

5. How do I order my priorities? Do I need to re-think my life and place things in proper order, starting with God and family, with other things to follow?

Concluding Prayer:

O Lord, our God, we have arrived at the end of our journey and our goal has been met. Our Lenten journey has taken us from the desert, to the mountains, to the hill of Calvary, and ultimately to the great triumph of Jesus' resurrection. Your son's triumph over death has brought all of us, his contemporary disciples and followers, the possibility of rising with him to eternal life with you. We pray that our journey this year, and the spiritual benefits it has reaped for us, can become part of who we are each and every day of our lives. The lessons we have learned, the challenges and hurdles that we have negotiated and the opportunities we have taken to spend time with you, have been worth every ounce of our effort. We now ask that the new spiritual norm for us be one that manifests a deeper and more profound understanding of you and a more fervent desire, through prayer and good works, to truly be the people you call us to be. The resurrection bids us to find a similar sense of new life in our world. May this greatest of Christian celebrations start us in a more positive path that leads to a permanent and deeper relationship with you. You are the source of our life. Through your son Jesus' rising to new life we too can find life without end. May the resurrection change us forever. Amen.

Afterword:
The Journey Of Lent: What Have We Accomplished?

We began this journey of returning home some forty days ago, but what have we accomplished along the road? If we have taken the message of scripture seriously and pondered its meaning in our life, then undoubtedly we have been challenged in many great ways. Initially, we were challenged to not fear this time of preparation, for there will be many hurdles that come along the way. While no one wants detours and obstacles, and there is certainly no need to seek detours and obstacles in our lives, they will indeed come. If we are open, however, we can see that such detours generally teach us significant lessons about our lives. If we engage rather than run away from such obstacles, the benefits can be significant. We have been encouraged to seek transformation in our life, not on the outside which is transitory, but on the inside where permanent and positive change can move us in the proper direction toward our eventual return home to God. We have been tested by asking what we need to do to promote our relationship with God. What needs to be rooted out of our life and what needs to replace it? What are the forms of darkness that must be cast out and replaced by the light which only Christ can give? Our Lenten journey has also confronted us by teaching that the paradoxical nature of Jesus' life, that life comes through death, is in fact a reality and, therefore, something we should not fear.

Another significant accomplishment of our Lenten journey has been the benefits we have received from the study of scripture and the many discussions that have ensued. We have learned that the interpretation of scripture is broad and varied. The synergistic effect of people coming together and sharing their thoughts and ideas has reaped many positive benefits. Things that we did not know and ideas that we never considered were raised in our discussions, prompting questions and ideas in our own minds, and forcing us to review our own thoughts and ideas. We were forced at times to look inside and ask why we believe as we do or understand things in a certain way. In short, we were challenged to broaden our perspective. While there is no need necessarily and we may not have changed our own ideas or beliefs, the benefit of hearing others and discussing varied opinions is certainly significant. Let us hope that the benefits of our time together may continue to blossom and produce much fruit in our personal lives, our associations with others, and most importantly our relationship with God.